P9-CCD-391

ROCHESTER

THE IMAGES

PHOTOGRAPHY BY DEAN A. RIGGOTT

TEXT BY CHRISTINE JENSEN

For the Bartlesons
Merry Christmas '97

Dean Riggott

DEAN RIGGOTT PHOTOGRAPHY
ROCHESTER, MINNESOTA

Special thanks to the following people for their help and support with this project:
Jim and Brenda Riggott, Don and Kathy Riggott, Jennifer Mueller, Marjorie Michaelson, Ethan Hyman,
Jerry Olson, Doris Mott, Randi Kallas, Dawn Irish, and Nadine Blacklock.

I would also like to thank the following businesses and organizations for their help and cooperation
with this project; Aquarius Nightclub, Assisi Heights, Barnes and Noble, The Broadstreet Cafe,
Chardonnay Restaurant, Daube's, The Federal Medical Center, Gold Crown Limousine, IBM, John Kruesel's,
Lanmark, Inc., Mayo Foundation, Michaels Restaurant, and Olmsted County Historical Society.

The following sources were consulted in preparation of the text: Rochester Area Economic Development, Inc.
(RAEDI); Rochester Convention & Visitors Bureau; Rochester Area Chamber of Commerce; *Mayo Roots* (Clark W.
Nelson, 1990); *Rochester: City of the Prairie* (Harriet W. Hodgson, 1989); *Rochester Sketchbook* (Val Webb, 1997);
Rochester Area Visitor (Rochester Visitor Publishing and Printing Company, May 5, 1997); *Welcome to Rochester*
(Post-Bulletin Company, April 1997); and the Division of Communications, Mayo Medical Center.

Credits
Art Direction: Dean Riggott
Photography: Dean Riggott
Design and Layout: Denise Walser-Kolar
Text: Christine Jensen
Printing: Doosan Dong-A Co., Ltd., Korea

Copyright ©1997 by Dean Riggott

All rights reserved. No part of this work may be reproduced or used in any form by any means - graphic, electronic, or mechanical, including
photocopying, recording, taping, nor any information storage and retrieval system - without written permission from the publisher.

ISBN 0-9659875-0-7 $18.95 (Soft Cover)

Published by
Dean Riggott Photography • 306 8th Street N.W. • Rochester, MN 55901 • (507) 285-5076

Rochester: The Images books are also available at discounts in bulk quantities for premium or sales promotion use.
For details contact Dean Riggott at the above address.

ACKNOWLEDGEMENTS

*I would like to thank the following individuals without whose effort and support
this book would never have been realized.*

My father, Don Riggott, who inspired me to become a photographer
and for the support and guidance he has given me throughout my life and my career.

Jerry McCullough, former photo editor of the Rochester Post-Bulletin,
who gave me my start in this profession and to whom I owe many thanks.

Jerry Olson, chief photographer at the Rochester Post-Bulletin,
whose guidance, support, and inspiration have been invaluable to my career.

And Jennifer Mueller for the love and support
she has given me throughout this project.

ROCHESTER, MINNESOTA

For natives and newcomers alike, the city of Rochester offers an array of memorable images. Some probably think of the giant Canada geese nestled on Silver Lake, half-hidden by the early morning mist. Others might think of the oversized ear of corn that stands guard over the intersection of U.S. 14 and 63, or the city's distinctive skyline, anchored by the downtown buildings of Mayo Medical Center.

The land that is now Rochester was once part of the Chippewa and Sioux nations. In 1854, pioneers George Head and Thomas Simpson stopped in this part of the Minnesota Territory and staked their claims on the shores of the Zumbro River. The settlement that grew up around these first homes was named "Rochester" after Head's hometown of Rochester, New York. In four short years, the population had grown to about 1,400 settlers, and the city was officially incorporated.

With the help of a railroad connection, Rochester grew to be a thriving agricultural center by the 1880s. The now-famous Mayo family was already part of the community by this time; Dr. William Worrall Mayo had arrived with his young family in 1863. During the Civil War, he was an examining physician for the Union Army Enrollment Board. After the war, he set up his own medical practice and later, he and his two sons planted the seeds for what was to become the world's largest association of physicians in private medical practice.

Today Rochester is the fifth largest city in the state with a population of almost 80,000. The city's strong economy is built around health care, computer technology and agriculture. The 1990s brought a cascade of recognition for the city, including being named by *Money* magazine as one of the top three places to live in the United States for five years in a row. Over the last few decades, the city's population has steadily increased and become more culturally diverse. A strong economic base is important, of course, but the city offers much more: exceptionally clean air and water, more than 60 city parks, outstanding public and private schools, and amenities usually found in a much larger city.

Situated about 40 miles north of the Iowa border and 75 miles south of Minneapolis/St. Paul, Rochester is the business and cultural hub of southeastern Minnesota. An international airport on the south side of the city is the gateway for a large number of visitors from other parts of the U.S. and abroad. They come for medical reasons, for business or for other reasons, and their presence gives Rochester a cosmopolitan flavor. Celebrity visitors in recent years have included the Rev. Billy Graham, former President Ronald Reagan, Jordan's King Hussein, Barbara Bush, Bill Cosby and Arnold Palmer.

There was nothing famous about Rochester when Dr. W. W. Mayo arrived in 1863. Born in England in 1819, he came to the United States as a young man and worked his way West as a doctor, veterinarian, surveyor, newspaper editor and boatman. Along the way, he married Louise Wright who assisted with his medical practice and managed her own successful millinery business. Weary of moving, it was Louise who insisted that the family stay put in Rochester after the Civil War ended.

The couple had five surviving children, three daughters and two sons. William James Mayo was born in LeSueur, Minn., in 1861, and Charles Horace Mayo was born in Rochester in 1865. Both joined their father's medical practice after graduating from medical school. "Dr. Will," as he came to be known, received his training from the University of Michigan, graduating in 1883. "Dr. Charlie" graduated from the medical school at Northwestern University in 1888.

The year of Dr. Will's graduation was pivotal in Rochester's history. On August 21, 1883, a tornado devastated the city, leaving about 30 dead and hundreds injured and homeless. At that time, there was no hospital or organized medical care available in the community. The Sisters of St. Francis, a Catholic charitable teaching order, helped the local physicians care for the injured and homeless in the wake of the disaster. After the crisis had subsided, Mother Alfred Moes, leader of the order, approached Dr. W. W. Mayo with the idea of establishing a hospital in Rochester. At first he declined, but Mother Alfred was persistent. When she and the sisters offered to raise the necessary funds, he agreed to help her plan the facility. Saint Marys Hospital was established in 1889. With 27 beds, it was the first general hospital in southeastern Minnesota and the first in a series of medical institutions that today make up Mayo Medical Center.

In 1892, the three Mayo physicians began to invite other physicians to join their growing medical practice. Each doctor had a specialty, but they combined their skills for the benefit of each patient. This principle of "group practice" remains the hallmark of Mayo today.

The elder Dr. Mayo died in 1911 at the age of 91, just one month after he and Louise celebrated their 60th wedding anniversary.

In 1919, Dr. Will and Dr. Charlie turned over their personal assets to form what is now Mayo Foundation--a charitable, not-for-profit corporation--and the entire medical staff became salaried. The group practice continued to grow under this new structure and in 1939, the one millionth patient was registered. It was also in 1939 that both brothers died.

What made the Mayo brothers so famous? Both were skilled surgeons and caring physicians, but they were much more. Both were lifelong students and teachers; both were civic leaders and philanthropists. Their insatiable curiosity led them around the world in pursuit of new ideas which they adapted to their own medical practice. Word of medical "miracles" spread, and patients began to travel to Rochester from great distances. Some of these patients were famous personalities whose presence attracted additional attention. Physicians also traveled to Rochester to learn, leading to the development of the world's first graduate medical educational center. More than anything else, however, the Mayos and their partners were widely recognized for their ability to diagnose and solve an array of difficult medical problems.

The Mayo practice continued to grow throughout the century. The first Mayo Clinic Building was completed in 1914 and was built on the corner of First St. and Second Ave. S.W.--formerly the site of the Mayo family home and today, site of the Siebens Building. In 1928, the Plummer Building was opened; at the time, it was the tallest building in Minnesota. Saint Marys Hospital continued to grow to keep up with the burgeoning Mayo practice, and in 1954, the so-called "downtown hospitals" that also supported the Mayo practice were incorporated as Rochester Methodist Hospital. The following year, in 1955, the Mayo Building was completed, although at the time it was only 10 stories high. In 1966, Rochester Methodist opened what is now known as the Eisenberg Building-- unique at the time because it introduced a new floor design for hospitals, the radial unit. By 1970, the Mayo Building had added eight more floors. These are just a few of the many construction projects undertaken to support the growing medical practice over the years. In 1986, Mayo Clinic merged with the Saint Marys Hospital and Rochester Methodist Hospital to form Mayo Medical Center.

Today, Mayo Medical Center occupies more than 10 million square feet of space in about 40 buildings, making it more than twice the size of the Mall of America. Mayo provides comprehensive "one-stop-shopping" for the diagnosis and treatment of virtually any medical problem. In a typical year, about 250,000 patients register at Mayo Medical Center; this translates to about 1.5 million patient visits (individual meetings with physicians) annually. The expertise of Mayo's 1,150 physicians and scientists spans more than 100 medical and surgical specialties and subspecialties. At any given time, there are about 1,600 residents and other students at Mayo Medical Center; total staff is about 18,000. Together, Saint Marys and Rochester Methodist hospitals provide more than 1,900 beds and almost 90 operating rooms. The combined total of surgical cases performed each year is about 45,000.

In 1986 and 1987, Mayo Foundation expanded outside of Minnesota with the openings of Mayo Clinic Jacksonville (Florida) and Mayo Clinic Scottsdale (Arizona). In 1992, Mayo began to form a network of health-care providers in the region surrounding Rochester. Mayo Health System now includes clinics and hospitals in about 50 communities in southern Minnesota, western Wisconsin and northern Iowa.

FULL MOON OVER MAYO AND GUGGENHEIM BUILDINGS

Much of the Mayo history has been preserved through buildings and artifacts that can be visited or viewed today.

Directly east of the Mayo Building stands the Plummer Building, which provides space for patient testing, research, support services and a medical library. The restored offices of Dr. Will and Dr. Charlie also are preserved there. Designed by Dr. Henry S. Plummer, an early partner in the Mayo practice, and Ellerbe Architects, the building remains as interesting and appealing today as when it was completed in 1928. Take, for example, the solid bronze outer doors that face Second Ave. S.W. Each door weighs 4,000 pounds and bears detailed raised designs depicting life in Minnesota. The doors remain open except for ceremonial closings, such as when the Mayo brothers died in 1939 and when President John F. Kennedy was assassinated in 1963.

The distinctive bell tower on top of the Plummer Building houses one of the largest carillons in North America, originally consisting of 23 bells. In 1977, the range was increased when the descendants of a Rochester pioneer donated 33 more bells. Carillon concerts can be heard by any passer-by on Monday evenings or during the noon hour on Wednesdays and Fridays.

Another beautiful building on the Mayo campus, but diminutive in comparison to the Plummer Building, is the Mitchell Student Center. Situated directly south of the Mayo Building, at the foot of the Guggenheim Building, this small but elegant stone structure was designed by Rochester architect Harold Crawford and completed in 1937. For 35 years, it housed the public library. When the city library moved to larger quarters in 1972, the building became home to Mayo Medical School, established in September of that year.

Much of the personal history of the Mayo Clinic founders has been preserved through the homes of Dr. Charlie, Dr. Will and Dr. Plummer. These family homes also served to house and entertain the growing number of physicians and dignitaries who traveled to Rochester in the early part of the 20th century.

Dr. Charlie was an avid agriculturist and conservationist. He and his wife, Edith, built a country home for their family and called it Mayowood. The 50-room mansion, built in 1910-1911, is on Mayowood Road S.W. and was home to three generations of Mayos. Besides the home, the 3,000-acre estate included stables, barns and a greenhouse. As busy as he was, Dr. Charlie found time to establish a model dairy operation at Mayowood that helped set local standards for milk production. In 1965, Dr. Charlie's descendants donated Mayowood to the Olmsted County Historical Society which continues to maintain the home and offer tours to the public.

Dr. Will and his family built an English-style manor house in 1918 on what was then the outskirts of town--just a stone's throw from the site of the pioneer brick home of Rochester's founder, George Head. As Dr. Will's wife, Hattie, worked closely with the architects, Dr. Will made only one request; he asked that the plans include a tower similar to the one in his parents' home from which he and his mother had studied the stars. In 1938, the Mayos donated their 47-room home to Mayo Foundation as a meeting place where people in medicine could exchange ideas for the good of mankind. Known today as Mayo Foundation House, the home serves as the setting for Mayo staff dinners and educational functions.

The genius of Dr. Henry Plummer was showcased not only in the Plummer Building, but also in the home he built with his wife, Daisy. The original site in the "Pill Hill" section of Rochester included 65 acres. (The nickname "Pill Hill" has to do with the fact that so many doctors built homes in the neighborhood.) The home, completed in 1924, included some unusual features for that time: an intercom, a central vacuum-cleaning system and the first gas furnace in Rochester. After Dr. Plummer's death in 1936, his widow continued to live there until 1969. At that time, Daisy, a concert pianist and patron of the arts, donated the house and 11 acres to the local art center. Three years later, ownership was transferred to the Rochester Parks and Recreation Department. Known today as Plummer House of the Arts, the home is open for public tours and is the setting for hundreds of parties, meetings and weddings throughout the year.

Another pivotal year in Rochester's history was 1956, when Thomas J. Watson, Jr., then president of IBM, announced that Rochester had been selected as the site for a major new IBM plant. Ground was broken later that year, and the distinctive blue plant in northwest Rochester, just west of U.S. 52, opened two years later.

The decision to build a plant in Rochester has had a profound impact on the city and surrounding area. With the plant opening, IBM created 1,750 new jobs. By the late 1990s, the plant employed almost 5,000.

At first, more than 20 different business machines were manufactured at the Rochester plant, but over time, the focus shifted to development. In 1988, IBM announced that the Rochester plant would be responsible for developing and manufacturing its AS/400 models. These mid-sized, multi-user business computing systems are the most popular of their kind in the world.

Today, IBM Rochester is recognized as one of the company's most efficient plants in the world. The Rochester plant won the 1990 Malcolm Baldrige National Quality Award which resulted in a steady stream of national publicity for the Rochester team.

A number of other high-tech industries also are located in Rochester, for example: software and service companies such as Showcase Corporation and Metafile Information Systems; Western Digital, a center for computer disk drive research and development; and PEMSTAR, a contract manufacturer. Other local manufacturers include: Crenlo, a metal fabricator employing more than 1,000; Waters Instruments, producer of medical and farm products; and Telex, a manufacturer of communication equipment such as hearing aids.

While there can be no denying that health care and high-tech industries are powerful forces in the local economy, there is a third and equally important player: agriculture.

Agriculture and agribusiness account for fully one-third of the jobs in Olmsted County, of which Rochester is the county seat. Farms in the area produce annual harvests of corn, soybeans and a variety of fruits and vegetables. Employment at Seneca Foods Corporation, as well as other plants, swells in the summer months as corn and other vegetables are processed. The giant corn-shaped water tower at Seneca Foods is a Rochester landmark, although it no longer serves its original purpose.

The area's dairy farms yield more than two million pounds of milk each year, and Rochester is home to Marigold Foods, maker of Kemps Ice Cream. Other large dairy-producing plants in the county include AMPI (Associated Milk Producers, Inc.), Pace Dairy Food Co., and Land'O'Lakes. Also, a meat-processing plant, Rochester Meats, Inc., employs about 250.

The valley in which Rochester sits was attractive to early settlers because the land was fairly level, the topsoil was fertile, and the underlying sedimentary rock provided good drainage. In Rochester's earliest days, potatoes were the major crop. But the Civil War greatly increased the demand for wheat, so in the late 1800s, wheat became the most popular and profitable crop to grow in this area.

A tour of the land surrounding Rochester today reveals the present-day diversity of farming activity: a variety of crop farming, dairy farming, orchards, and specialty farms. Sekapp Orchard, on the east edge of town, and Kelly's to the north, are especially popular in the fall when families start looking for pumpkins, apples, gourds and bittersweet. A Sunday afternoon drive reveals a number of small farms where llama, sheep and goats are raised. From spring until fall, two outdoor Farmers Markets draw crowds by offering specialty meats and dairy products, organically grown fruits and vegetables, fresh-cut flowers, bulbs and seedlings.

There are a number of other businesses and not-for-profit organizations that contribute to the character of the city.

A thriving hospitality industry takes care of Rochester's more than one million visitors each year. The 55 local hotels, combined with restaurants and other hospitality businesses, provide jobs for more than 8,000 people. Largely due to Mayo's presence, Rochester has more than 4,600 hotel rooms--far more than is typical for a city its size. Several of the larger hotel properties are owned by Kahler Corporation, an organization whose history dates from the 1870s and is intertwined with that of Mayo Clinic. During the clinic's earliest years, John Kahler responded to several requests from the Mayo brothers to convert hotel space to hospital space. Kahler got out of the hospital business when Rochester Methodist Hospital was formed in the 1950s.

Increasingly, conventions account for a significant share of activity in Rochester's hospitality business. Since the Mayo Civic Center was completed in the 1980s, convention traffic has steadily increased to about 75,000 in 1996. The expansion of the skyway system has made the city even more attractive to convention-goers during the winter months.

Another important characteristic of Rochester is its tradition of excellence in public and private education. In the southeastern corner of the city lies the beautiful campus of University Center Rochester. The campus is home to three institutions of higher learning: Rochester Community and Technical College; University of Minnesota, Rochester Center; and Winona State University, Rochester Center. These institutions cooperate to offer a wide range of diploma, certificate and degree programs. Rochester also is home to Minnesota Bible College and the educational arm of Mayo Foundation, which includes Mayo Medical School, Mayo Graduate School, Mayo Graduate School of Medicine, Mayo School of Health-Related Sciences and the Section of Continuing Medical Education/International Education.

Also in the southeast quadrant of the city is the Federal Medical Center. Patients were first treated on this site in 1879 when the Second State Hospital for the Insane was opened. The specialized hospital was known for many years as the Rochester State Hospital. Most of its buildings were constructed in the 1950s, but the hospital was closed in 1982 due to a decline in patient population. In 1985, the facility was reopened as the Federal Medical Center. Today it is one of only a few such medical centers nationwide providing inmates in the Federal prison system with medical, surgical and psychiatric care.

Perched on a hill in the northwest quadrant of the city is Assisi Heights, motherhouse of the Sisters of St. Francis. Founder of the community was Mother Alfred Moes, the friend of Dr. W. W. Mayo who convinced him that Rochester needed a general hospital. In cooperation with the elder Dr. Mayo, Saint Marys Hospital was established in 1889, and the Sisters of St. Francis initially provided its funding and nursing staff. Their involvement with the hospital continues today through the Saint Marys Sponsorship Board. Assisi Heights, built around 1950, is a beautiful example of Italian Romanesque architecture, similar to the Franciscan convent in Assisi, Italy, where their patron saint was born. Sisters from Assisi Heights have taught and served in schools and health-care facilities throughout the world. Since about 1970, Assisi Heights has been available as a site for retreats, workshops, educational functions and solitude. Public tours also are offered.

Scattered throughout the city are about 90 houses of worship, representing 40 religions, denominations and sects. The oldest of these structures is Calvary Episcopal Church, located in the heart of downtown Rochester, right across Third Ave. S.W. from the Mayo Building. Established as a parish in 1860, the cornerstone of the chapel was set in 1862 and the church was consecrated in 1866. Other buildings have been added since then, including a parish hall designed by Harold Crawford. The picturesque courtyard provides a setting for outdoor concerts and other activities during the summer months.

Downtown Rochester experienced a rebirth of sorts starting in the mid-1980s and extending over a period of about 10 years. Like many cities across the country, continued movement to newer neighborhoods on the outskirts of the city had left a quiet and tired-looking downtown. The heart of the city is a lot less quiet these days.

The completion of Mayo Civic Center in 1986 kicked off an impressive series of construction projects that continued through the mid-1990s. Among those structures are the Kahler Plaza Hotel, Radisson Plaza Hotel, Galleria Mall, Centerplace (an office building), Peace Plaza, a new Government Center serving the city and Olmsted County, a new public library, fire station, and numerous skyway connections. The skyway system, combined with the Mayo and Kahler pedestrian subway system, makes it possible to walk throughout the entire downtown area without going outdoors.

During the same period of time, Mayo also undertook a number of major construction projects. The Siebens Building was erected just north of the Plummer Building, and the Charlton Building was added just west of the Rochester Methodist Hospital's Eisenberg Building. Floors were added to the Guggenheim, Hilton and Baldwin buildings, once again altering the city skyline. About a mile west, aging facilities at Saint Marys Hospital were upgraded, and the Mary Brigh Building was greatly expanded. New buildings also were added, including the Generose Building which houses the Mayo Psychiatric and Psychology Treatment Center. In 1996, a hospital-within-a-hospital opened at Saint Marys: the Mayo Eugenio Litta Children's Hospital.

As if that weren't enough construction activity for a city of Rochester's size, a major flood control project along the Zumbro River worked its way through the city over the course of several years in the early 1990s. The catalyst for this much-needed project was a major flood that occurred on July 5, 1978, after six inches of rain fell steadily on rain-soaked ground. Five people were killed, and more than 5,000 Rochester residents were evacuated from their homes. As part of the flood control project, the river channel was widened and deepened, a number of dams were built, pedestrian bridges were replaced, landscaping was improved, and new biking and walking paths were built along the river. When the project finally was completed in 1996, the U.S. Army Corps of Engineers awarded the city its single annual Award of Excellence.

In the midst of all that is new, much of the old has been saved.

For example, the Olmsted County Historical Society has preserved one of the county's oldest dwellings, the Dee Cabin. Built in 1862, it is said that 25 men put up the poplar-log cabin in one day. Shoemaker William Dee, his wife and four children lived there for 15 years.

In the downtown area, just east of Charter House in Central Park, stands Heritage House, a living museum depicting life in the mid-to-late 1800s. This house was built in 1875 by Rochester merchant Timothy Whiting and was moved to its present site in 1972. This classic Victorian farm home has been restored by Heritage Associates, Rochester Park and Recreation Department, Eden Garden Club and other interested individuals. Near the house, also in Central Park, are near replicas of the original park fountain and band shell.

A sentimental favorite in Rochester, the old Chateau Theatre, was saved from the wrecking ball when it was refurbished in the early 1990s to house a Barnes & Noble bookstore. Built in 1927, the Chateau was one of the most elaborate in a succession of movie theatres built in Rochester in the early 1900s. Its unique "French village" decor included interior balconies and turrets, and artificial vines and flowers on the stucco walls. On the ceiling above the almost 1,500 seats was an array of twinkling stars. In addition to motion pictures, dramas and vaudeville shows were staged in the theatre.

Many other older buildings have been adapted for modern purposes without sacrificing their historical charm and significance. Among them are the old Armory, now a Senior Center; a century-old Victorian home, now a restaurant; the Olmsted County Bank and Trust Building, now a microbrewery; the old Broadstreet Building, now home to two restaurants and several offices; a cluster of beautifully restored buildings on Historic Third St. that house a variety of businesses; and a similar grouping of historic buildings lining South Broadway.

When it's time to escape the hustle and bustle of daily routines and responsibilities, a person in Rochester doesn't have to travel far. The city maintains 60 parks covering more than 2,500 acres, which include 30 miles of paved walking and biking trails and 32 playgrounds. The parks' beauty and uses change as Rochester experiences four distinct seasons. Summer walking paths become cross-country ski trails, and soccer field parking lots become outdoor ice-skating rinks.

The city also maintains 12 other recreational facilities, including Quarry Hill Nature Center, Plummer House of the Arts, Watson Sports Complex, Rochester-Olmsted Recreation Center, Mayo Civic Center and Graham Ice Arena. The city offers three public, 18-hole golf courses, two with driving ranges, in addition to the three public, non-city owned golf courses.

By far the best-known park is Silver Lake, just east of the 700-1200 blocks of North Broadway. Silver Lake is home to one of Rochester's biggest attractions: the world's largest winter concentration of giant Canada geese. In 1947, a flock of 12 geese from Nebraska was released on Silver Lake by a former Mayo Clinic patient. The presence of these geese lured some of the few remaining geese of this type to Rochester. The following year, in 1948, the Rochester Power Plant began to use water from Silver Lake for cooling--a process that returned warmer water to the lake--and the geese began to spend the entire winter on the ice-free lake. The number of feathered visitors varies from year to year, with an estimated peak of about 30,000.

WINTER COVER AT SILVER LAKE

In 1962, visiting biologists arrived for routine banding and weighing of the geese. The biologists confirmed that there was something special about this flock. These were, in fact, giant Canada geese, a species believed to be extinct. They differed from Western Canada geese in that they had longer necks, broader bills, lighter plumage, a longer wingspan (72 inches), and a heavier average weight (12 pounds). The flock's nesting grounds are in Manitoba, Canada. The honking overhead that heralds their arrival in autumn is a welcome sound as the geese have become the city's unofficial symbol. The Minnesota Department of Natural Resources provides winter food for the geese with about 80 acres of planted corn in the surrounding area.

Silver Lake also offers canoe and paddle boat rentals, and a paved path for biking and walking.

For those who love the arts, Rochester offers an array of cultural activities including concerts, live theatre and art galleries.

Rochester Civic Music supports community bands and choruses, hosts the popular "Down by the Riverside" outdoor concert series, brings in groups such as the Minnesota Orchestra, and presents an annual Yule-Fest concert. The Rochester Orchestra & Chorale focuses on classical music but offers a few surprises, too, such as backing a 1997 concert by the Moody Blues.

Rochester Civic Theatre stages seven productions each year, two of which are aimed at children. The Rochester Repertory Theatre also mounts a full season of productions, and the Masque Youth Theatre and School provides training and performance opportunities for young people. There are also a number of private dance studios in Rochester offering classes for all age groups.

There are at least 10 art galleries in Rochester including the art collection of Mayo Medical Center. The Rochester Art Center on East Center St. offers a full schedule of exhibits, special events and classes for artists of all ages.

Other entertainment options include a variety of big-name performers brought in by Mayo Civic Center. Film buffs have their choice of 19 movie screens in the city, and local night spots feature a wide variety of entertainment.

Now join Dean Riggott as he takes you on a visual journey through this remarkable city. No doubt you will agree that this lifelong resident and seasoned photographer has captured some of the most unique and beautiful images that Rochester has to offer.

ASSISI HEIGHTS

DOWNTOWN ROCHESTER

PEACE FOUNTAIN BY CHARLES GAGNON

Mayo Civic Center

SAINT MARYS CHAPEL

SAINT MARYS HOSPITAL

WATERFALL MURAL (ZUMBRO BIKE PATH)

SILVER LAKE BIKE PATH

STONE WALL (MAYOWOOD ROAD)

CLUBHAUS BREWPUB (OLMSTED COUNTY BANK & TRUST BUILDING)

SILVER LAKE GEESE

MAYOWOOD MANSION

BARNES & NOBLE (OLD CHATEAU THEATRE)

RIVER CROSSING

PLUMMER BUILDING ENTRANCE

ASSISI HEIGHTS ORCHARD

PLUMMER HOUSE

KAHLER PLAZA HOTEL

MAYOWOOD GALLERIES

MAYOWOOD BARNS

PLUMMER BUILDING CARILLON TOWER

MAYOWOOD LAKE

Broadway Buildings

CITY HALL ATRIUM

APPLE TREE (ASSISI HEIGHTS)

RURAL ROCHESTER (COUNTY ROAD 8)

"MAN AND FREEDOM" SCULPTURE (MAYO CLINIC)

METHODIST HOSPITAL & CHARLTON BUILDING

BROADSTREET CAFE & BAR

"Constellation Earth" (Methodist Hospital)

MEMORIAL PARKWAY

HISTORIC THIRD STREET

Bluebells (Mayowood Trail)

MITCHELL STUDENT CENTER (OLD PUBLIC LIBRARY)

CENTRAL PARK FOUNTAIN

SILVER LAKE BIKE PATH

SEKAPP ORCHARD

SOYBEAN HARVEST

CHARDONNAY CUISINE EXCEPTIONELLE

OLD CITY HALL & HENRY WELLINGTON

CALVARY EPISCOPAL CHURCH

60

CHRISTMAS LIGHTS

SUNSET AT SILVER LAKE

Razor Wire (Federal Medical Center)

ATRIUM (UNIVERSITY CENTER ROCHESTER)

PLUMMER TOWER REFLECTION

KELLY'S ORCHARD

SENIOR CITIZENS CENTER (OLD ARMORY)

Dee Cabin (Historical Society)

QUARRY HILL

MAYOWOOD ROAD

MORNING SWIM AT SILVER LAKE

PAPPAGEORGES (MICHAELS RESTAURANT)

HERITAGE HOUSE (CENTRAL PARK)

AQUARIUS CLUB

Dr. William W. Mayo Monument

JOHN KRUESEL'S GENERAL MERCHANDISE

FOURTH OF JULY FIREWORKS

SILVER LAKE BRIDGE

MAYO FOUNDATION HOUSE

International Business Machines (IBM)

SOLDIERS FIELD GOLF COURSE

SENECA FOODS WATER TOWER

OLD FARMALL AT SUNSET

ROCHESTER SKYLINE

DEAN A. RIGGOTT

Rochester native Dean Riggott has worked as a professional photographer since 1991. Along with his position as a photojournalist with the *Rochester Post-Bulletin* and *Agri News*, Dean also specializes in stock and wedding photography.

Dean's passion for photography began on his 14th birthday when he received a camera from his father, Don Riggott, a professional photographer himself. Through his early years, Dean picked up valuable information from his father. He spent much of his time shooting nature and landscapes before shifting his focus to environmental portraits. In 1991, Dean did numerous photo exhibits throughout Rochester, and in March of that year was asked to join the staff at the *Rochester Post-Bulletin*.

Inspired by his father's release of *Norwegian Light* in 1982, Dean decided that a photography book of Rochester was a project he wanted to pursue.

The images in this book were taken over a period of two and a half years.

CHRISTINE JENSEN

Christine Davidson Jensen grew up in Butler, Pennsylvania, and came to the Midwest to attend Grinnell College in Iowa. After graduating from college, she worked in Iowa for nine years, first as a high school language arts teacher and later as public relations director for a small college. The years in Iowa also resulted in marriage and the birth of two daughters. Christine and her family moved to Rochester in 1985 where she continued her public relations career with Rochester Methodist Hospital and Mayo Clinic.

Today, Christine is owner of Davidson Jensen Public Relations, providing businesses and not-for-profit organizations in southeastern Minnesota with independent public relations counsel. She is accredited by the Public Relations Society of America and has an MBA degree from the University of St. Thomas. Christine is a full-service counselor whose special areas of interest include communication audits and strategic public relations planning.